ABC

That could be me!

Written by
Little Coleman

Illustrated by
Lindsay Scott

La Reunion

DALLAS, TX

A is for **Architect.**

Paul R. Williams designed buildings that stand big and tall.

B is for **Ballerina.**

Misty Copeland dances gracefully across the stage.

MARIE MAYNARD DALY
worked in a lab
with tiny molecules.

D is for **director.**

Oscar Micheaux
made and produced
many movies.

is for **Engineer.**

MARY JACKSON
helped put people
into outer space.

G

is for **Geologist**.

Marguerite Williams
studied the earth
we live on.

is for **Historian.**

Carter G. Woodson
studied African
American history.

I is for **INVENTOR.**

LEWIS HOWARD LATIMER made the light bulb shine brighter.

J is for **judge.**

Thurgood Marshall decided laws as a Supreme Court judge.

K is for
Kinesiology Professor.

Samuel D. Hodge Jr. teaches his students how the body moves.

is for **Lawyer.**

MACON BOLLING ALLEN
fought for what's fair.

M

is for
Meteorologist.

Charles E. Anderson
could predict
rain or shine.

N is for **Neurosurgeon.**

E. Latunde Odeku found and treated brain conditions.

is for
Opera Singer.

Marian Anderson
filled auditoriums
with beautiful singing.

P

is for **president.**

Barack Obama was the leader of the United States of America.

R

is for **Realtor.**

Philip A. Payton Jr. sold people their beautiful homes.

is for
Vice President.

KAMALA HARRIS
listens to the needs
of our country.

W

is for **Writer.**

ON MESSRS HUSSEY & COFFIN

phillis wheatley
wrote beautiful poems.

X is for X-Ray Technician.

William Edward Allen Jr. could see our bones through an x-ray machine.

Y is for **yodeler.**

mike johnson uses his voice to make cool sounds.